# *Magpiety*
## *New & Selected Poems*

*Melissa Green*

ARROWSMITH
PRESS

Magpiety: New & Selected Poems
by Melissa Green
© 2015 Melissa Green

Second Printing
ISBN: 979-8-9904050-6-6

Boston—New York—San Francisco—Baghdad—San Juan—Kyiv
Istanbul—Santiago, Chile—Beijing—Paris—London—Cairo—Madrid
Milan—Melbourne—Jerusalem—Darfur

11 Chestnut St.
Medford, MA 02155
arrowsmithpress@gmail.com
www.arrowsmithpress.com

The eighteenth Arrowsmith book was designed and typeset by Erica Mena
for Alex Johnson and Askold Melnyczuk using Arno and Baskerville typefaces.

Cover art © 2015 by E. Ian Maurer

*My four cardinal points:*
*Bill, Claire, George, and Marylinn*

## Magpiety: New & Selected Poems

## from *Magpiety*

## from *Fifty-Two*

## from *The Marsh Poems*

# From the Author

In the same way that Eliot's lantern throws the pattern of nerves on a screen, I see each of my books as connected to a psychic darkness that called out for a different articulation both in form and language. The torque in the lines corresponds to the contortion of a spirit in pain that gave rise to a lyric impetus I needed only follow out. Periods of creativity were interleaved with despair and years of writing nothing at all.

*The Squanicook Eclogues*, a long elegy for my father, was published by W. W. Norton in 1987 and was followed by a one year stay in Charles River Hospital. There, the beginnings of those stories that became *Color Is the Suffering of Light* began to make themselves known. The book, a memoir, was published by W. W. Norton in 1994.

The poems in *Daphne in Mourning* were written during the 1990s. The volume consists of formal elegies of varying lengths, many in response to the loss of my friend and mentor, Joseph Brodsky, who died in 1996. It was never published.

I was inspired to write *The Heloise* in a deep depression in 1984, and I knew it would take years to hone my craft enough to to turn the letters of Heloise and Abélard and their complicated history into a lyric novel of poetry and prose. I nearly had to invent a language that would stand in for Heloise's own vastly stocked treasure house, as she was fluent in French, Latin, Greek, Hebrew and possibly Aramaic. It was finished in 2011, and has not been published in full.

In 2005, I nearly lost my foot to an infection. After a long unpleasant recovery, I realized that my metrical foot had also been changed—the poems in *Fifty-Two* have a sharp break after two-and-a-half lines which replicated for me the sound of the snap of a Ticonderoga pencil. When I began my usual dense lyrics, I felt a kind of fracture in the language and knew I couldn't continue to write the way I always had. *Fifty-Two* was published in a limited edition by Arrowsmith Press in 2007.

*Magpiety* arose directly from the anonymous Renaissance poem "Tom O'Bedlam's Song" and with the call and response of the lesser known—and probably later—"Mad

Maud's Song." In order to write my version, I searched for language that had fallen out of English in order to invent a dialect for Maud's voice as she struggled with delusions, her dread of madness, of the loss of Tom, and of Bedlam. The poem's lines are very long, broken as if by her need to breathe and by a mind that kept wandering away from itself. The sequence was published in *Little Star* #3 in 2012.

*The Marsh Poems* was written under the ominous belief that it would be my last book. It was finished in 2011 and was never published.

*The Linen Way*, a memoir, was an attempt to braid together all aspects of my life: the mental pain, the history of my growth as a writer, and the central influences of Derek Walcott and Joseph Brodsky on my work. It was published in 2013 as an ebook by Rosa Mira Books in New Zealand.

I would like to thank my friends at Arrowsmith for their fierce attention and loving support: Askold Melnyczuk, Erica Mena, Jennifer Murphy, Mitch Manning, and Sumita Chakraborty. This is the second brilliant go-round—that makes you family.

from

# *The Squanicook Eclogues*

*(1987)*

# The Squanicook Eclogues

for Richard Winthrop Green, Jr.

## *April*

*i  from the sketchbook*

After a blustery, fretful March, the fields have yawned,
Tossing off their goosedown coverlets to thaw.
In airing upstairs farmhouse rooms, the sunlight paints
A sudden gold leaf on the dresser drawers and wall.
In his oldest jacket, I wade the oxen road,
And under my boots, a gingery leaf-fall breeds new growth
Beside the crooked stone wall bordering two states.
Heaved by frost, it holds its steady, snakelike course,
And now it's dappled in a shadblow's oval shade.
Brush-marked by spring, the sodden alfalfa is brassy with birds.
Hundreds forage in the bleached reeds, robins and starlings,
Striking like fired shafts from a branch's shuddering bow.
Beneath the russet mulch and leaves, a culvert floods
An aisle transfusing tender pergolas of grapes.
Clouds from the south scallop an altar cloth made by nuns,
And the loyal brass horse reels on the ridgepole spindle.

My father chose the iconography of trees
Instead of church, and on those Sundays, served the Truce
Of God. No argument divided us except
A war of grapes. What light artillery escaped
His lips was whistling so peaceful that it seemed
A sparrow's furtive mourning from its book of psalms,
Intended for the breeze alone; in spring, his scythe
Was steel instead of words. Chaotic April seethed,
In ruthless disregard for boundaries, across
Our forty-acre farm, a hummock at the crest
Of Barker Hill. Below, an amphitheater wide
And far into the valley from our northern woods,
A granite quarry like an ancient city slept
Submerged, and bright with runoff from Monadnock's slopes,
The drifting ash a hundred Januarys' snow.
Its wagon wheels were buried driftwood half-moons now.
And farther, past a line of conifer, the town
Lay huddled, unaware we watched, its houses strewn
Along the spongy inlets of the Squanicook.

*iii from the notebook*

The shadblow's white five-petaled stars have dropped in snow.
Elliptical bursts of bright green chevrons fan the air.
Along the wall, the linden fills with heart-shaped leaves,
Palmately veined, serrated, pale and olive green.
The willow is a yellow prairie sundress, fat
With catkins, a woman in a rocker shelling beans.
The maple's clustered fountain jets of blood have splayed
In short-lobed leaves, the stenciled veins of stubby hands.
In alfalfa, spiders have labored to weave the peat-rich air
Into goldenrod, daisy, geranium, trillium, lily, phlox.
Tentative teaberry rings its bell-shaped blooms.
*Anemone quinquefolia* fans attenuate stalks
Beside unfurling bloodroot, surrendering its white
Flags, a virgin banner on an emerald field.

The river dwellers claimed her: Eostre's men who caulk
Piazzas and their bulkhead doors; the boys who thrust
Aluminum canoes through currents past their wrists
In summer; widows' mottled ornamental ducks,
Oblivious to light from either equinox,
Reflecting gravely on their sluggish, perfect forms,
A travesty of Eden's flocks; eroding farms;
Displaced Triptolemus who wandered west and died.
Such an intermingling of dreams the brook endowed.

*v   Water*

Father, I'm drowsy in April's humming sun and think
A girl the color of autumn kneels at the Squanicook's bank,
Who is the river's daughter, dressed in driven skins,
Who knows a cedar wind at Nissequassick brings
The schools of alewife, herring, yellow perch ashore.
The Place of Salmon roars with light. She steps, sure-
Footed onto stone; lithe as a poplar, bends over
The water. Wren feathers, shells, seven quills quiver
In her sable hair. Her eyes, a spring-fed stream,
Like silica, seek bottom. Deep in her mossy brain,
The white-tailed mouse is born. She carries in her supple
Body all of spring—a tree frog in the apple,
A kit fox dozing in the brush, a brash otter
Diving her river-veins—the new, young, utterly
Green morning beads her skin. How simply she leans
Into understanding, baptized by light and the delicate lines
Of shadow from cedar. A goldfinch has flown its ribbed nest,
Dusting her cheek with its wing, a hummingbird throbs in her wrist,
She is drenched in waking. Wonder, a long-legged doe,
Drinks in deeply, as all instinctive creatures do,
And laughs, leaping the current, printing the field with dew.

## *August*

I thread the blackberry thicket for the shaded stone.
August has shriven the grass, the green sargassos of June,
And summer's alfalfa is lusterless gold in a nimbus of heat
Waiting the baler. It wavers, helpless, a phalanx of light.
August drums as bright thunder trumpets the field,
And the maple's khaki undersides lift in a brisk salute
To shadows stalled against the pitiless scope of the sun.
Rain will riddle the valley, strafing blistered grains,
And black-eyed Susans in unison rise like the girls of St. Anne's.
Where foxglove in her petticoat has crowned the hill—
An indolent cotillion girl who tosses gold
From her shoulders, and proudly rustles yards of crinoline—
Freckled goldenrod assembles, choir boys,
A drift of anise, bobbing over their schoolyard gate.
A sunflower's ovate leaves become the rough arms
Of a drowsy field hand, leaning on a split-rail fence,
Whose mouse-brown eye, alerted, lashed with gold, translates
The clouds as victory, the wind's voice as rain.

I knew the river wasn't theirs at all. Just once
When January sun on snow had made us wince,
When hickory and juniper were frosted cakes
On Barker Hill, my father traced the Squanicook
With one gloved hand above the valley's heart—a braid
Of shattered mirrors bridging fields and barns and roads,
Through yards resigned to her encyclical despair.
In watching shards fragment those stalwart gabled spires,
I saw a fractured picture of our town and knew
I heard an ancient, urgent fury break the snow,
A fierce quicksilvering of winter's crusted dyke.
I watched it runnel gently where we crouched; its wake
Defied the valley, joyfully sped from where we gazed.
I felt the shrugging off of nature's deep disguise.
The river favored us. She lived and leapt the gorge.

*iii  from the notebook*

The shadblow sheds its purple fruit and spills its seeds,
The linden bartering yellow bouquets for a necklace of gourds.
Unbraided pennons, catkins of the willow, fill
Like ragged sails. A towering cumulonimbus patrols
The eastern skies. I watch magenta clover drone
On sleeping epaulettes and know the sun-soaked earth
Is breeding still: in torpid pools, in stagnant ponds,
Rebellious nature sets her offspring quarreling
For food and territory—inbred stoneflies riot
For their rations where the water striders run
Their useless marathons; inflammatory toads
Attempt a revolution, all in vain. In time,
The planet's microscopic battles merge and fail,
Leaves of drying blood consumed, a season's compost.

*iv*

We walked the property a thousand times, as if
Without our walking there, the landscape might dissolve.
His trees were young. A drought-summer spark had cleared
The western third some time ago, and when he could,
He meant to have that forest back. He planted spruce
The size of children's pencils, fifteen hundred sprays
Of evergreen, each year as spindly as the last.
It hurt to watch him tearing up the ones he'd lost.
We carried water from the brook sometimes. It sluiced
A dozen clotted paths, where once an ancestor sliced
The forest open, and oxen, yoked, had dragged a road.
This was ours. New Hampshire, north of us, was broad
And diffident as France. With vague disdain, at six,
I knew our woods were better—even my burdocked socks
Belonged to Massachusetts. And I loved our field
Whose hundred-year-old hair had not been cut; it filled
With captivated birds. A thorny orchard kept
A dozen wizards prisoner. I watched their script
Of runes engrave the granite sky with ancient debt.
Everything the woods could teach, my father taught:
Delight, exactitude, a faith, his journeyman's doubt.

*v   Fire*

Father, I'm dizzy in shimmering August, rising new
As summer's mistress from a field of corn. She now
Is married to the heat-swept grain. Her ripening breast
Is a thicket, bright with blood berries, her body dressed
In flame. The red god of the salamander sandals her foot,
A monarch touches her lip, her coppery hands fit
Petals in a chain. She knows she has chosen to burn
At noon, as nature intends. The thrust maize, unborn,
Has made her heavy and drugged as a bee. A tawny wood
Dove sleepily croons what her tongue cannot: the subtle wound
That too much plenty makes. She doesn't know that winter
Ravages, that grief and habitual wind will tint her
Skin and break the tender stalk of her body. She stands
Impaled by arrows of afternoon light until thunder stuns
Her—she slips like smoke into shade, behind the burning stones.

# October

*i from the sketchbook*

An early frost has lathered alfalfa's stubbled cheek,
The oxen road crunching like bacon under creak of my boots.
Another flawless Sunday in October, clear,
Crisp, a pure sky plumed at the border by woodsmoke
And pagan banners of trees beguiling Protestant spires.
All the harvest has come down the valley: shelves
Protesting under bushel baskets, barn after barn.
The staghorn sumac rears its bloody hooves against
The ell where grapevine bickers with its shadow self.
Ceremonious maples don the cardinal robes of kings
While the dowager dogwood embroiders her taffeta cape.
Two starlings quarrel in an alder's blazing arc,
And for a moment, all the trees are winged, as if
In rousing autumn, a thousand bright tanagers, tiered,
Ruffled their breast feathers, calling. They cannot settle here.
Across the bronze medallion, dusk, a skein of scarves
Draws the wild geese over, audibly mourning, hoarse,
High wings turning the wheel of our envy, our grief.

More than novelty crooked its finger—silent, austere,
Deeper than trees beating their wings or the purblind stare
Of a black snake circumscribing a sapling's wrist.
Father carefully penciled facts, describing rust,
Habitat, genus, disease, but his meticulous chart
Of change didn't teach me to name the woods' mysterious heart.
*Father, I'm frightened. Why are things so beautiful and sad?*
My voice had dusted moss, like snow, without a sound.
Stern and tall, he cupped his chin. As if in pain
He paused, then reached into his pocket for a pen.
*Don't ever make things up. Write only what you see.*
*Name the woods and you'll have named the world,* he said.
He tore some pages off and handed me his pad.
I heard the current crimp, mimetic, on the pond,
And larch or beech or birds murmuring over me. The task
Was how to write *birch* when I saw the crumbling, pale tusk
Of a fallen mastodon bridging the path, or *ash* when the air
Was frenzied with the head of a neighbor's rain-black mare.
Sycamore waved at me like drowned Ophelia's hair.

*iii  from the notebook*

The shadblow shivers like a saved corsage, bronze
And apricot powder dusting every palsied leaf.
A spinster of chicory fearfully clasps a lilac stalk
With virginal fringe, guarding her single-day's bloom.
The clans convene: more coarsely toothed, in heart-shaped leaves,
Resilient, wrinkled aster skirts a hardihood,
The meadow filled with cousins who were towheads once;
Canadian thistle resisting a curvature of spine
Beside a boggy culvert; boneset, crowds of dock,
Replacing ragweed neighborhoods with random vetch.
A westerly wind shuffles the linden's pack of cards,
Held in age-spotted hands at a hennaed game of whist.
Witch hazel, worried by a joiner's planing hand,
Uncurls its shavings, branched like dowsers' wands, in vees.

*iv*

Something stirred from sleep as we passed by. It woke
And shook itself, I saw it light the linden's wicks
And heard it leafing through a coded archive, heard
An earth-brown collared killdeer beat its feathers, hard.
I knew the spirit of a thousand seasons rose
To welcome us, so long in coming through the trees.

*v   Earth*

Father, leaves she's sent out from her leather hand,
A skulk of foxes, cannot turn the hunter's hounds.
October's temperamental wind, which burned to seize
The tamarack and rowan by their bridles, sighs
Because they're fetlock deep in thorns. She is so old.
She can't outlast the transpiration of her blood.
And from a fire-fed bough, its flame, an ember the color
Of lynx, she's a bruised husk shaking the woods, a collar
Of yellow corn crowning her shoulder. Her fingers fret
Her belly, a swelled calabash that bears its fruit
Too late. She rests her cornucopia in frost
To sweep the chaff away, too tired to protest
The vagrant beggary of bats, the fossiled sky.
Her limbs erupt in ivy's epochal decay.
What is a body but a bier? Or suffering but love?
She gathers cones for her own barrow, takes down leaves,
And like the marrow-colored moon in clouds will guard
The huddled valley's harvest of beliefs. A gourd's
Faint staving-off of evil is rattling for God.

# January

*i   from the sketchbook*

The jays are commissars in uniform that rule
By evolution's ordinance. Its lesser birds
Survive haphazardly: the wrens are refugees,
And robins following the railroad south have veered
Toward destitution's camp, where fields are deeply scrolled
And hushed by January's harsh regime, and skies
Consolidate to cobalt under tungsten clouds.
A stenciling of dendrites drawn in photogravure
Has marred the gray horizon. Now consumptive twigs
Display disease and poverty across its screen.
In drifts, the muffled trees like soldiers shake their coats,
Elbowed in bark as in gabardine, and curse the wind,
Rabbits fraying their cuffs, trailing threads away.
The valley's shadows dust the snow with powder blue.
A crow concealed in arborvitae gives the charge,
And thorns like firing pins repeat it, lifted limbs
Defy both weather and the order to submit—
A stand of minutemen, bareheaded, stamping for dawn.

*ii*

My father solemnly believed a God could live
Articulate in sumac and arbutus leaves;
That daily witnessed death could be outrun
If once observed and written down. In sun, in rain,
I learned that duty and devotion walk together. As the stream
Diverged, we stood on separate banks. He tried to show
Me where a red-eyed vireo might nest, the shy
Elusive whippoorwill might hide, but I could not
Distinguish anything except the wildest note
Of pity in their singing.

The shadblow's winter bark is grayish-green, and arcs
A double helix skyward like a double stair.
Its slender, ruddy, three-pronged twigs are mulberry
And beige, no bigger than my smallest fingernail.
The linden's lesions, caused by fungus and decay,
Have fissured vertically, the claw marks parallel.
And rusty dogwood, tiled in ragged, reptilian plates,
Is sparring with its fuschia-colored, knuckled nodes.
The basket willow's tasseled catkins dangle in defeat,
Its twigs unraveling a yellow-greenish yarn.
The black trunk of a beech bristles its thousand wicks.
Today is a daguerreotype, tinted and brittle with loss.
Light dims the field. My fisted hands burn.
The crow shuffles its wings, arches over, is gone.

*iv*

Palpably, the day
Was going. Twilight spilled the sky's embankment, dyed
On cloudy rungs cascading heaven's water wheel.
I saw the shadows joining hands, and all the while,
My father stood bewildered under Hesperus
And seemed to pray, I heard the birch's aspirates
Decline Monadnock's name; his, I think, and mine.
What called us? Was it me or something live that moaned?
He would not answer. Sickness burrowed every limb.
Our walks would fail. There was no resurrecting him.
But I have kept on walking, being tutored twice:
My father's daughter, trying to be spare, precise;
A child of earth, insistent on hell, on paradise.

*v   Air*

Father, she's made the wolf a widower and orphaned us.
The world lies ruptured to the root, its harvest crushed
By her fallen heel, a maddened heaven thrashing white
Across her unforgiven dust, and shrouded elms weighted
In mourning. She who is dead teaches us grief, grieving
For us with a seraph's prayer and stylus, whose all-engraving
Trance transfixes us. Sleep has taken her up
Into its branches. She lets fall her shredded hope
Of treaties with the earth, regretting every flake's
Surrender. Dreamless in the shriven heart of oak,
Her thin, diminished breath collects until the day
When star lichen studs the bark, a junco and chickadee
Will bear her back awake, willing herself young
Again, unpinning her hair, the river's rising song
Reviving us with mercy, in the water's tongue.

## The Housewright's Mercy

for Rick and Joyce

I heard the apples softly letting go
at summer's end, and knew abundance drowsed
beside me in the field, her freckled arm
flung wide above her headscarf, while a dream
of cider filled the Nonesuch cheeks with rust.
They tumbled from her apron, fully grown.
A sparrow, mating with its echo, bred
a fledgling music. I was no one's bride.

Who knows why summer broke my heart that year?
September always said, *Too ripe, too ripe.*
In Hubbardston, the world was threshing gold,
my brother's acres far too light-beguiled
for herds or harvesters. And who could reap
the hillsides, flecked with such excelsior?
Oh Lord, I couldn't pray, as language asks.
I was too small, and autumn's immaterial husk.

And when some worm deranged itself in me,
I thought I couldn't live to watch the light
inevitably yield. A thread, a hair
was all that held me to the earth that hour—
invisibly plucked from her golden head, she laid
redemption in my hands. A scythe might mow
the meadow now. I saw that both my life
and death would matter less than any leaf.

I sat alone, an anvil's shadow, as
five workmen pounded on my brother's house.
Their awkward, fitful battering on brick,
on granite, pinned me to the apple bark,
their hammers thundered wood the way a horse's
fired hooves bombard its stable doors.
I heard in their harangue of wrists a flash
of judgment, and their gavels nailed my flesh.

A pause. Then on the scaffolding I felt,
like rowers straining toward some far-off shore,
their purpose forge a single instrument,
I heard *one* hammer's rhythm, adamant
with joy—it found the root of work in sheer
exertion, making, as the rafters filled
with iron on the clapboards' stave, both song
and signature where men have moved as one.

And as they beat in harmony, I thought
a cloud of sawdust half-eclipsed the sun.
The hammers slowed to match my heartbeat while
their shapes upon the ridgepole dimmed. And veiled
by cooler, unfamiliar light, with sand
the mind can worry pearlward in my throat,
their restoration stood for all we make
in life, and all that perishes like smoke.

*ii   The New House, 1802*

I saw how Joseph Wright would heft his axe,
Wachusett, Asnacomet, Burnshirt Hill
still wilderness, his Great Farm Thirty-Two
a parchment blot, a Monarch's dribbled tea.
He'd trace two Georgian parlors, limn a hall,
an ell, his carriage shed and barn. With sticks
to mark the corner posts and piers, he'd pace
an arch where wagonloads of hay would pass.

He'd hear the oxen snake a sawyer's sledge
through clotted undergrowth, his timber roar
a snowy skid way to the stack, where sills
were hewn and sawn a season later. Soil,
uncovered by the carted oak and briar,
in bloom with every limb his team dislodged,
would flake with cedar wood chips to his shins.
He'd watch the drawshave's resin gild his hands.

The master mason's shyest son would smoke
a beehive oven, full of firebrick,
until he dropped. But stung because the Dutch
were libeled there, he'd dig a man-sized ditch,
then supervise the cradling of rock,
each hoisted hearthstone guided by his stick.
He'd blush and bend to lift his palanquin
of clay. They'd use his tempered bricks, in quoins.

The mason, topping out the chimney course
and waving like a weathercock, would toss
his trowel down and drop his scutch and hod.

His chimneys pointed heavenward. They had
proportion. They would conquer even trees.
Extinguished at the firedogs with cares
of men, the wood and not his flues would fail
when sparrows, nestling in the thimble, fell.

And though they knew their carpentry was good,
the men would flinch to think he'd find a flaw,
and wipe their boots, afraid to enter rooms
that they themselves had built. He'd diagrammed
the balustrade and stairs. The wainscot. Floors
of twenty-two inch pine, like planks of gold.
He'd thumb the latch, a man afraid to wake,
and touch his tricorn, grateful for their work.

She'd stand, like Ruth among the gleaners, broom
in hand, to clear the shavings' chaff from wheat.
Their house was built. A landlocked brigantine.
The hipped roof. Elegant. The downspout, turned
where fascia boards and soffits met. The weight
of stories borne by joists and summer beams.
He'd proudly stroke a pilaster. Then carve
his *Boaz*, just above the fanlight's curve.

*iii  The Widow, 1819*

But building such a house would kill him. Now
I see their marriage candle—Martha Wright
would rock in her bedroom window, facing west,
for twenty years without him and would twist
her hair, a braided flame, in figure eights,
entwining all the sorrows women know.
The moon in poplar trees, her ivory comb,
a world away, she'd weep as evening came.

When Joseph Wright wed Martha Eveleth,
*briefly, briefly*, as the fiddler sang,
the apple trees themselves wore periwigs,
and crows in frock coats settled battles waged
by cedar fencepost statesmen, witnessing
their declaration of intent. A myth:
it was not fruit that tempted Adam but
the deeply moonlit orchard's featherbed.

Thus passion's mill wheel ladled out their Sabbaths.
On fevered linen, spent by love and quarrels,
as quickly as she healed, her body writhed:
their blue-eyed Joab, Aaron, earnest Ruth;
Chloe, Sally, Nathan, Bildad, Charles;
the babies, quiet Catherine, Dorcas, Beth.
What piercing joy to have it all again:
his whisper *moppet*, then her lying-in.

They grew like summer saplings while their hair,
those fields of wheat the wind might gently part,
would darken at the milk room door. She'd chalk

their crowns, her fingers tethering their cheeks,
and measure what another season spared.
How good God was. And then she wasn't sure:
her fallen willow Sally flailed a week;
her first-born Joab struck down like an oak.

Mortise-and-tenon. Post-and-beam. She'd trace
her husband's drawings in her sleep—a home,
a virgin house, a ghostless place where plagues
of earth would never come, a farm built leagues
from grief. In Hubbardston, the saw pit hummed
where mists at evening through the trees,
her fevered logic like an invalid's,
were children, by the elders, being led.

Crocus. Cowbell. Leaf-fall. She'd mistake
each season's alchemy for happiness.
Their first December froze so deeply, graves
could not be dug. The cistern of her grief
encased in stone her daughter Chloe, next
to Joseph, dead within a week of stroke.
I see a tundra through their window cracks,
and northern lights, still burning as she rocks.

*iv*

Her widowhood was one long labor, piled
like cordwood in the shed. Her patience streamed
through fallow fields, on sun-struck corn, a scythe,
in geese disconsolately going south.
A miller, plowman, smith and cooper stormed
the farm, her full-grown sons; her daughters pulled
down linen, fresh from apple boughs, to press
the housewright's relict back to earth, in peace.

I thought I saw the clapboards pale, as though
the house itself could mourn for Martha Wright,
but it was snow, a thousand nor'east gales
that blew above a shipwreck—furied gulls
new generations of neglect had brought.
The timbers groaned. The shingles warped with thaw.
Defeated by its never-ending chores,
no legal owner was his rightful heir.

His hayfields stand like beggars at the gate
and startle reptiles in the ferns. The roots
of one remaining wineglass elm succumb
as ivy splits the shattered fanlight's cames.
A shutter bangs. Powder post beetle routs
the summer beam where Queen Anne's lace forgets
itself and leans like Puritan children toward
a gibbet or a pulpit or their God.

I knew what Joseph Wright had known, what drove
each handmade nail: *no marketplace could price
such beauty. Sons must fence themselves apart.*

But through the dusk, his vision half-impaired,
empowered by the things of earth to praise
the earth, the housewright saw our love, derived
from his; who chose this lifetime's enterprise,
as artists' work—by work—is best appraised.

My brother wants a visionary's house,
and reads and signs the housewright's master plan:
in what we leave behind, a chiseled script,
we ask for mercy's constant care, to keep
our names alive. This verse I've tried to plane
for strangers, hewn as faithfully as his,
this home I build, the labor of my life,
must be a place in which the world can live.

Who knows what heaven is? Or if we're left
with Joseph shouldering his ax, the girth
of ringed infinity's elm—to try and glimpse
through darkness Martha's incandescent lamps.
Does broken Carthage most resemble death,
or do those workmen on the roof who lift
a horizontal beam, stripped to the waist,
still forge the final crosspiece of the West?

from
## *Daphne in Mourning*

*(2000)*

## A Sea Change

The fever of August has stormed itself out.
Bouts of sweat and fury have blistered me weak.
Wrack, rock, seaweed disentangle and tangle the shore.
Surely I didn't used to wash my glasses so often.
Afternoons crumble underfoot like shredded wheat.
What a genius I have for confusion.

My handwriting belongs to someone else.
Alzheimer-like, crab-wise, I take down this dictation.
A titian-haired cocker spaniel named Lizzie
Dazzles me, never leaving my side. Anxious. A rescue dog.
Dragged back, I don't know where my home is either.
*Mother, you won't believe how dark the dark is.*

St. Francis received the first stigmata.
Mata Hari wore silk and duplicity like mine.
Mindful of the steps, I write these splintering words
as swords of light hang from the eaves like ice.
My eyes still know winter when I see it.

## Leda, Later

Remind me: my bed is empty,
my graying hair pinned up
and tumbling from a starfish clip
where once a waterfall by Crivelli flowed
over the white shoulders of Sparta.

I do not quarrel with my warring children.
Their bad marriages are their own affairs.
I sit on the rocks and watch the waves,
my toes now horny as a tortoise's.

*That night a storm came off the sea.*
*I saw St. Elmo's fire electrify the spars*
*and a bluish current quivered on my skin.*
*I studied my egg-shaped oval in the glass,*
*breath like a wing beat in my throat,*
*wind tearing white curtains, my flesh,*
*and feathers on my bed in flight.*

I am an old woman writing poetry.
I never wanted intimacy with goddesses
or gods, never wanted their dangerous progeny.
I only dreamt of passion, possession,
surrendering to the torque of human love.

## A Sparrow Fostered Elsewhere

its wings frosted, lost
above the wrong continent,
faints in the Arctic air,
conveyed, half-conscious,
from current to current
over the blinding tundra below.

Under a white crag
above a whiter river,
a flotilla of ice floes churns
the chilled banks,
chiseling minuses there,
and water, seized by the cold,
seems to change into an ancient self,
as if into a longed-for transformation
to be beautiful and eternal:

*marble*, from the bright glacier of Carrara,
the veined and burnished, sweat-polished
shoulders of slaves that turned and became
colonnades of Illyrian villas;

*marble*, the rose-dappled tiles in the Temple
of Diana at Ephesus where the youngest virgin
dips an ivory toe in the petal-flecked pool;

*marble*, quarried and laid end to end
on barges to expand an empire, sailing
south through the Sea of Marmara to Anatolia,
north through the Bosphorus, sledding

through gilt and birch-whiteness to St. Petersburg
for the bath of a Czarina.

To be well used. To endure.
To make or be made the beautiful.
Buffeted at the edge of the known world,
over a river riven with ice—
the shards of my heart
as seen from the air—

I am not rock or rib,
cathedral or ruin,
only the tiny
five-pointed star
fragmenting
the sparrow's watery eye.

## The Vigil

I've dug my grave before I die
and wait for my war dead there
all night, braiding my hair by the hour.
The anorexic moon is tired.

The Squanicook is listless, crimping
silently between gaunt trees,
damp air fingering my dress,
the grass where the dead are camping.

I hear old guns embattling fields
and see the lowliest soldier mount
and ride the carbon decades, mined
with stars. The blood-black sky is felt.

Hoof prints spark the bridled sea,
a froth of surf enchains her mouth
as Wilfred Owen, turning north
through Massachusetts, climbs to me.

He jumps the battered iron gates,
dismounts, his tunic buttons light
as fireflies, his epaulettes
shivering as he vaults the graves I guard.

Past cenotaphs of angels, lambs,
the skull-and-willow patterned stones,
he stops before the twentieth urn
where a maiden in relief is limned.

He presses my marble cheek
against his *Croix de Guerre*. His lips
awake me from my anxious sleep,
his breath a mist of sea spray, smoke.

"My dear, you read me back to life.
My rhymes, in your lovely mouth rehearsed,
surprised me out of death. I heard
you whisper, *Wilfred, you must believe*

*you did not die at Sambre Canal.*"
But now in his voice the shrapnel splits
my heart, the hurt that buried him a pall.
He shivers as if he felt the shelling's nails

of lead could still be falling, a fusillade
of golden ingots to injure us,
his eyes the greenish murk of gas.
I lead him away by the hand like a child.

The woods weep out their foliage,
the Squanicook wrapped in midnight's crepe.
We lie down beside the river's edge.
Covered like lovers in leaves, we sleep.

An ivory cameo carved by war
in morning's light looks rouged by love.
My kisses are the sutures where
his wounds and pallor both dissolve.

He lost his color far from here.
My faith has made him fair again.
I tug up his collar, tuck in his hair,
both nightmare and its terror gone.

"Owen, go, it's time you rode
the withes and raddles of your verse,
your language luminous and vast.
Recall sometime your virginal bride."

His eyes are topaz, strewn with stars.
"I'll never leave you, wife," he grins,
and bareback, boyish, grips the reins
and gallops through the scalloped bars.

I wave him off, I wave him home
by daylight, still in a limpid dream.
Who enters poetry's vaulted realm?
Under my breath, I have his hymn.

Embracing death, I take my life
in mortal hands, where pain is bound
by tourniquets of joy, and bones
that calcify, unbandage love.

My eyes agleam with viruses,
my human voice with its sweet stench,
the suppurating none can stanch—
I'll liquefy with mysteries.

Language made my longing free
and caught it. Who smells the whiff of ichor?
My body—both a skiff and anchor,
the carious rose, its curious fire.

A cloud's hands move to eclipse
the eyes of the young day moon.
The Muse is faint. The angels mourn
their fall—the sounds a baby lisps

are more divine and never leave
the ear of God. East winds rise
and ruffle up the underbrush.
I sit beside my grave and laugh.

The dead are vigilant. They wait.
Carved out in Braille, my hands caress
their metaphor and rhyme, erased
by not a minute since their deaths.

Brodsky's cigarettes still burn
like lasers through the paper birch,
and Papa's rifle scope and scotch
can crack the best prose ever born.

Frost's folksy scythe will surely mow
a man down like a blade of grass,
and Hardy's gentle breath outgusts
a blizzard on his bleakest moor.

Lorca's ancient lyrics catch
on sword point young Europa's bull;
and Dante's eye transfixes a full-
blown rose of light a Mendel couldn't match.

At noon, in no man's land, I pledge
to whet my knife on polished tomes
the dead have left, no stone unturned.
My pen point stabs and stabs the page.

The littlest lark is whistling through
the boughs. My song is tearing now.
Tomorrow it begins anew:
my violent loves, their overthrow.

## Daphne in Mourning

for Carol Moldaw

Palm fronds have woven out the sky.
Fog has infiltrated every vein.
My hair has interlaced with vines.
Cobwebs lash their gauze across my eyes.

I've stood so since the world began,
and turned almost to stone some years ago.
Who passes by perceives a lichened post,
my girlish features, ghostly, nearly gone.

My bark is warmer than the dead's.
Human blood still lulls the underside of leaves.
My fingers hold the very dress I loved
to dance in, when dancing mattered—and it did.

## Hic Jacet

Hide my grave
From turncoat grief

Let autumn storm
My lichened stone

And no one come
To call me home

Let shadows pass
And winter's priest

But no one make
A chisel's mark

Nor dates surround
A hyphen's rune—

Horizon line
The country lane

I traveled on
Afraid alone

I moved stone walls
By granite will

And made the road
A boulevard

A highway nosed
The wilderness

A thoroughfare
Paved over fear

My loving fed
A silver flood

A river raced
Where my heart rose

My footsteps drummed
The stairs of dreams

My whispered tears
Connected stars

A bridge of words
An ocean wide

My human voice
Once entered space

A cobbled song
I sang to God

## Portrait of an Artist

His coat of many colors ebbed to green,
a muddied delta where the spectrum ran
into the sea, as if all rose and sandalwood
had been redeemed for prophecies of grain;
the olive of a copper faun in ruined
Rome behind a colonnade of weeds.

New England burned. We talked about our lives.
October traveled seaward, and it cleared.
He winced, in match light, at my shyest praise,
and domed with wisdom like that tyrant's slave,
paraded through a fierce tobacco cloud;
a beardless Job ungoverned by surprise.

I shivered, watching him. The other guests
were dancing in an upper room, while jazz
kept winnowing the ashes on the hearth.
I nearly wept to hear the humble ghosts
of fricatives that fled his lips—a Jew's—
and Russian-English vying for his breath.

I might have said, *You've made our deserts bloom,*
*the plagues are passed, your brothers will atone,*
*oh have, my heart, the patience of the earth.*
But Love, afraid to speak, could never blame
his turning on his orphic heel, a caustic tune,
percussive, sifting ashes on the hearth.

## Matryoshka

My words perish
in the reed's parish.

This beetle's carapace
is no surprise.

A Russian doll encloses
independent clauses,

a blood-embroidered egg
candling the wounded age.

Remove the tattooed shell,
reveal what scriveners hold:

a seed, a heart, overfull
of the world since Adam's fall.

# A January Poem
### January 28, 1996

*i*

Joseph, I pounded on the studded door of the sky
with my palms, not believing you've closed it
behind you forever, the midnight black mahogany
paneling of a private club where all the dead—
and only the dead—are welcome.

Inside a smoky, book-lined room,
you're playing cards at a green baize table
with Wystan Auden, your beloved mentor
and (her archaic smile like a kore's) Tsvetaeva,
and you are chortling into your cognac,
"I'll see your sonnet and raise you a terza rima,"
trying to explain the pun in the line
"Paradise—it's nicer than Nice"
to the young waiter Chatterton
in a white apron serving canapés.
The nine Muses step from their lunettes
in the ceiling of clouds, calling for Pan.

People have come so far to celebrate.
Mandelstam has gathered his bones
from the snowy transit camp near Vladivostok,
and pressed his first new suit in ages.
He enters the parqueted library, limping
on the arm of Nazheda, his long-suffering wife,
and Akhmatova, your champion, regal
as an Egyptian Queen in her paisley drapes from Paris.
You step forward to embrace them all.

A genial host at his own party, you show them
shelves of gilt and leather bindings
between rose ogival windows, excitedly exclaiming
to Mandelstam, unable to resist the pun:
"See here, they've bound all your writing, Osip—
one full of poems, the other of gossip."
And M., still speechless from the grave,
can only marvel at his work, so many volumes
printed by ibis and cranes, hawks and egrets,
turned into books in their own tongues.
Wystan and Marina come to stand beside you
to watch the starlight startle your Black Sea.

Under the eaves, on a white table,
a candle whispers into its glass hands.
There on the summer wicker furniture,
still dressed in their coats and hats
from the long train journey,
your mother and father sit beaming.
Those brass buttons twinkling yet,
open toward you like that avenue
near the Neva, and for the first time you weep,
going down on one knee between them,
kissing their palms with your tears.

And then your heart swells to think you can make
this wide veranda, the terraces and vineyards
down to the sea and beyond, into that infinity
you dreamt of in the days you laughed together—
before you knew the brightness of Rome,
or had the canals of Venice carved on your heart—
when you three lived in a room and a half.

*ii*

Outside, the world is unaware that you have died.
A blizzard is throttling Boston and New York.
At St. John the Divine, two thousand tapers are lit,
one from the other, a slow migration of Cyrillic
and sibilants, moving east to west as you did,
and one by one your living friends, drawn
and trembling in the bands of your death,
mount the podium to read a favorite of your poems,
each intoning like a priest a well-loved passage
from the Book of Common Prayer—your work
the congregation knows and can recite by heart.
A susurrus of sighs quivers through tongues of flame.

I too was supposed to climb those high steps
like a pilgrim to read *I was in Rome. I was flooded by light,*
my hand trembling over the place on the page
where Dante's P's were once engraved,
and the fan from an angel's wing
had cleansed them, leaving only a luminous scar,
but I was not able to travel from my own internal
prison—I was snowed on my pallet, stunned for all
who would never be soothed. For the poems
death had taken from us. For the man she'd taken.
I thought even language itself might be weeping.

Once I was too sick to live
and you came to my bedside
with all late summer in your arms,
a vast bouquet of pinks, golds and greens,
a trace of earth and birdsong.
You wrapped me in a blanket
and held me like a child on your lap,
a ghost in my own life.
We didn't speak for hours.
Not a tear was shed.
Your breath on my cheek was so moist
it sank into my too-thin skin,
and my pulse began its faint resurrection.
Your erratic heartbeat slowed to measure mine.
We sat all afternoon together
like some twentieth-century piéta—
two refugees consoling one another,
you in exile from your country,
I apart from myself.
After you'd gone they carried me
to the Quiet Room, torn with sorrow,
the sheet they covered me in
cold and light as a winter snowfall.

Nothing made of glass was allowed on the ward,
so the nurses divvied up your glorious flowers.
Ranged around my room for days
in the only vases they could find—
ten blue plastic male urinals—
would have made you laugh out loud.

It was all the autumn I was missing, and all of you.
Two weeks later, you won the Nobel Prize.

The blossoms hung on. One afternoon,
the charge nurse sat on my bed and blushed,
abashedly took my by-then warmer hand.
"Your friend," she stammered. "I didn't know—
the day he came, it was before visiting hours—"
She paused and blinked, her voice ragged with chagrin.
"I sent him away like a *common tradesman!*"
I smiled for the first time in weeks.
You'd have liked her pretty discomfort
and being mistaken for one of the honorary poor.

As I write this, years have passed,
and it's as though you've just left the room,
the white bullet casings of filters
broken off your deadly cigarettes
crowding an ashtray, Handel's
*Watermusik* on the turntable,
the needle soundlessly raised
above the groove out of grief.

I have so much to tell you, Joseph.
I'm beginning to write well.
And the dark is darker than it's ever been.
I imagine you at a plain oak table
still smoking by a rainy window,
writing poems we wouldn't understand
because you know everything now
about time and space, your metaphor
and rhyme blooming in both—
no, in *every* dialect.

*v*

The caravansary arrives, a ten-line
Christmas poem, unburdening itself
under date palms in the desert, blown
sand peppering my eyes. Joseph, save

me as you used to! How am I to feed
these quarreling Russians, interlinears
dressed like émigrés, my alien drafts—
a feud of consonants and vowels? What kind of Ur

language do I need to know in order to help
pitch their tents, settle the camels, make
comfortable the women and babes, a bazaar of shapes
and syllables, in mufti, caftans, yarmulkes, yashmaks,

burnoose, and khakis, fighting to be heard
above the din of the millennium?
                                        It is a poem
about the Holy Family journeying over potsherds
into exile, a country you also traveled, the spume

of the Baltic salting your brow. I've never crossed
such a desert, Joseph, as this fiery trajectory—
the arrow of your going. Ahead of me, always from the crest
of a far-off dune you beckon, leading me, heartsore, teary,

into the future. How could the horizon curve away
without you? Metaphors dazzling as oases, your rhymes
like signposts star the heavens to lead us home, but we
are still in Egypt, Joseph, where your footprints are.

## *Flight to Egypt*
### from the Russian of Joseph Brodsky

… where the drover came from, no one knew.
Their affinity made the heavens slate
the desert for a miracle. There, they chose to light
a fire and camp, the cave in a vortex of snow.
Not divining his role, the Infant drowsed
in a halo of curls that would quickly become
accustomed to radiance. Its glow would climb—
beyond that dark-skinned enclave—to rise
like the light of a star that endures
as long as the earth exists: everywhere.

## *Reply to Styron's* Darkness Visible

*i*

Styron, it was violent, yes—
but a slower smothering. My eyes
became their own blindfold,
concussed by the light's chaos.

The velvet affliction spread.
The paralyzing universe sprawled.
My ears were clogged with cotton.
My nameless enemy prowled.

Like Daphne, I grew bark
and froze, mid-leaf. I broke
apart and did not fall
or feel the rain's rebuke.

My heart, an anvil, cracked
my ribs. The bloody creek
in my body ceased to run.
I curled in my crib to rock.

A glacier calved, true north
novocained beneath
the overwhelming sea.
My prayers interlaced with froth.

The dark not dark enough,
I deeply thrust my knife.
Murdering God. Myself.
And, gratefully, slaying love.

The tribes first flee the city.
An exodus precedes the Party
as rats run ahead of the plague.
My room reads No Entry.

Escaping partisans
pelt the guards with stones.
A river of inhuman sounds
makes refugees of song.

Children, whimsy, wild-
eyed women choke on words,
shot by the border police:
my lexicon of wounds.

Under evening's tarp
the dispossessed are stopped—
beaten, starved, now sleeping,
their page-white skin in strips.

          I could not hold
my mother in my arms. She was a mirage,
a ghost in Queen Titania's mask,
the sheer rock face of an eroding cliff.
Nothing grew above the tree line.
Every year, more of her slipped into the sea.

          I could not hold
my father in my arms. He was a tempest,
a tidal bore; sky-cracking lightning
flew from every fingertip. His voice
thundered through the valley of our hearts.
Terrible, the flooding of his face.

          I could not hold
my sister in my arms. She was an alley's
vanishing point, under which a sewer ran
and rats in heat. A streetlight shot out
for sport, she was a pattering of needles
like the rain, a place where girls like me,
found nude, are stabbed so many times
the knife blade's broken off.

          I could not hold
my brother in my arms. He was pastureland
and granite stonewalls that ran away from me
for miles through old oxen roads and woods,
a chainsaw razing stands of pine and ash,
the pounding engines of his farm machines,
a caller of sheep who seizes a fiddle by its throat,
melancholy seesawing in his chapped hands.

                    I could not hold
myself in my own arms. I was anti-matter,
absences, a tornado's swath of ashen dreams;
a country cemetery sown with death's heads
and willow-chiseled stone where all the names
are scoured out by storms, no more than
a glossolalia of consonants and vowels
disappearing on a sweat-stained page.

                    I could not hold
life in my own arms. The French clock's sweet
chime at the quarter hour; a grain of beach sand
caught in my eye soon wept out into wheeling
galaxies, where notes of Mozart winged their way
from clouds, an arabesque of stars; brush strokes
of Cézanne; scraps of pure color littering
the atelier floor as Matisse set his cut outs free;
Palestrina's masses encoded in my cells,
and Larkin's gorgeous glass of water
held to any-angled light, and all my pills.

*iv*

It comes over me like the whiteness
before a faint, a dizzying
embrace of fog
winding itself sinuously,
sensuously,
the length of my body,
like a ghostly anaconda,
the mist of its breath like a kiss
of anesthesia.
I feel nothing,
not even the slow
impending paralysis.
I have shed my body
like a light summer robe.

Birds wing slowly past
the window panes,
taking music with them.
Like a pulled plug,
all sounds drain away.
The French clock ticks
and stops, its sweet chimes
covering their mouths.
Every lovely word or kindness
I've been given evaporates
like morning from a pond.

Those who care for me
are suddenly estranged,
arranged like pictures at an exhibition,

unfamiliar faces fading
in unfamiliar frames.
The walls bleach, become
translucent, color leaching
out of the sky, the room, my eyes.
The fog has shrouded me.
I am clean in my glass coffin.
Without the world, I am free.
Pills like fresh water pearls,
a dazzling scalpel,
the heavy coil of rope
of my own hair,
I am fearless.
Weightless.
Resolute.

*v*

Nourish me, anguish.
Grief, become
my honeycomb.

Carry me, fury.
Ford the river
of my terror.

Swaddle me, sadness.
A crucible stores
my fiery tears.

Cradle me, sorrow.
Cloudless dawns
my eiderdown.

Mother me, darkness.
Lightly be
my lullaby.

Cover me, silence.
Stars, accompany
my liturgy.

*vi*

Wrapped in linen like a scroll
I retch with death, the godless scald
of suicide, deep hieroglyphs a child
would make blooming on my body as it cools.

*What kept me from my dream of being killed?*

Reluctant as Lazarus, and weak, I crawl
from the moldy cerements and scowl,
scratching my current-tonsured skull
in disbelief, faces and their daylight cruel.

I am brought back. Condemned to live in a cell
where once my wordless hope was scratched
in blood: to describe the earth, grow fierce and old,
all because, I think, my savior language called.

*vii*

Who called me from the frostbite of the street?
Who wrapped me in blankets when the conflagration died?
Who filled my mouth with honey when the taste
                of arsenic was all I knew?
                      Only you.


Who etched the rules for reckoning the crooked and the straight?
Who helped me measure coffins for the dead?
Who felt my bones, with a tender finger traced
                the calendar of scars I drew?
                      Only you.


Who yanked me from the bomb site, half-destroyed?
Who battered back the wharf rats of my doubt?
Who bathed my ravaged face of all distress,
                disorder, discontent with feverfew?
                      Only you.


Who chiseled out the lyrics lodging in my throat?
Who served cuisine a prisoner could eat?
Who led me to the cliffs so I could trust
                in distance, depth, the wings I grew?
                      Only you.


Who hummed the notes my ear could orchestrate?
Whose saturated palette painted out my dread?
Who taught this wild child how to speak and dress
                in human raiment and its sovereign hues?
                      Only you.

My thorax caked with blood again,
I am too old to bloom into a butterfly.
What Egyptian chrysalis wraps me in irony now,
a froth of winding sheets mouthed by moths?
What vengeful, virginal love assures
those brittle veils still drape the furniture?

Not love at all, but habits of abandonment:
mold and dust, mildew, dirt and grime.
These suffocating rooms have made me sick.
Who could stand the windows painted shut,
unopened gifts forgotten guests once brought,
the left-to-fester flowers in vases
crazed by a life that never came?

I've taken off the gloves and bodice,
the filigree of gossamer made by nuns.
I step before the cheval glass and stare.
Appalling, how those spider webs
have made their imprint on my flesh,
though all the clocks in the parlor were stopped.
*Help me, someone, unclasp this noose of pearls.*

*ix*

Sunlight routs the musty burial shafts.
Lace at the window whitens, breathes and luffs.

The newel post and balusters, oiled,
shimmer like a castle's palisades. Chilled

before the hearth's sudden glorious blaze
and the piano I test for jazz and blues,

a joyous riff of *a capella* scales
falls from my eyes, coins of the realm that scald

my cheek and brighten on the pitted floor.
I am richer today than in the flower

of my youth, richer than Croesus' wife.
Consonants and vowels I clung to all my life,

clean cotton bandaging my wounds,
I sign commitment papers—for the *life* I have won.

I am paler than ice.
A band of molten silver
cinches all my fears.
What do I do now—
now that I've seen my Ur-Sorrow,
saw where lightning
sizzled and stunned
the split heart of an oak,
my soul by force divided,
and the lightning long past?

Chaos perpetually stormed inside my skull,
adrenaline searing thoroughfares
throughout both hemispheres,
from whose rustling verges
my fox-colored thoughts
fled harriers and men,
darting through thickets,
thorns and undergrowth,
my tongue aflame.
I've hurled my body
through whirlwinds in fright.
I have no template for peace of mind.
Will witnessing this ancient breach
give me a human pulse at last?

Can I pass now at an ordinary pace
the incrementally budding pink
in a trio of crabapples on Crest Avenue
to enter my neighborhood coffee shop

for a muffin, *The Boston Globe*, and calm?
And if I walk to the edge of the sea,
will it teach me to stand still,
the steady pounding of horses
coming in, legions of waves arriving
to crash and collide on the seawall,
only a splash of new surf baptizing me?

I write my name on a white page.
So *this* is who I am.

from
# *The Heloise*

---

*(1984-2012)*

## Matins

At eight, I murdered God at Argenteuil.
A chaffinch, half-impaled on thorns, cried
and beat against my bloody hands until
her wound was deeper than her will to fly.

Silence filled the grotto where my prayer
had died. Such a light and fatal lance.
Such a patient fury in the briars.
The world went on, malevolent, immense,

spun by a fearsome God who wouldn't save
a sparrow. Sunlight, starlight, darkness burned
in my hot tears and through my fingers' sieve.
There was no God. And I had not been born.

~

They dolved my mother's cophin when I was five.
But at Argenteuil, I had a hundred mothers.
The nuns nantled me with kisses, governed me
with love, fed me on sculsh and sugared flawns

while I ran wild through the leas and holmes,
unfettered as a young deerling in bare wet feet
until one day to my astonishment the small black
daughters of Cadmus linked hands, and I began

to read. Sweat broke out on my brow. Little pagan
that I was, I had been given a wound, a holy gift,
worshipping devoutly thereafter at my first altar,
never dreaming there'd be another called Abélard.

# Lauds

I needed to study with a living Master. Paris
burned with learnèd men, but I wanted only
the most famous—the handsome, charismatic
dangerous Breton, whom Bernard of Clairvaux

accused of corrupting all the youth of Europe.
As this lickspittle traveled from duchy to duchy,
storms of boisterous students in his wake shouted
for bread, for ale, for dice and whores, disturbing

burghers and bishops, rousing pious virgins who began
unlatching more than gates; at larksong, deflowered,
drowsy, tearfully kissing at the back garden Abélard's
students, and chirming them out to the streets to sleep.

Older Masters were allwholly agged their pupils
flew to him, this acolyte of the anti-Christ. I heard
*Abélard, Abélard* when I stood with my basket
at the market; *Abélard, Abélard* luffed in the treen,

rustled in the book stalls, in the papershops, *Abélard,*
*Abélard*. At Mass a blush rose so violently, I was sure
not veil nor my damp palms in prayer could mask it.
*Abélard, Abélard*. I heard from an upstairs window

a girl's laughter spiral into a long bright piping,
astounding me, and when nature braided that cry
with a deeper one, and one song seemed to come
and climb from the same throat, I ran blindly home.

~

I gazed all summer at the rippling Seine slipping
away, the moon which rose to wash her red-gold hair.
When the housekeeper and I went to the fish pier,
I thought to look upon him, Abélard, or find his boys

around him like a chattering swarm. I didn't know
Abélard had already seen me, intending to harry me
to the ground as a deft wolf a lamb. When I begged
and Uncle agreed to let me be taught by Abélard,

I trembled in Notre Dame's cathedral close,
amiddleward a throng of outeners brabbling
in sheveled Latin, their student gowns *outremer*,
all of us impatient for Master Peter to appear.

Who was this warrior who had pecked the eyes
and vitals of the older Masters, defeating them
with his dialectics and quickness of mind?
He made enemies as fast as friends, simply

by stepping up to speak from a church porch
to lusty bellows and cheers. When I saw him
first, I wasn't moved, though the marble rang
and echoed with shouts and the crashing of fists

against slate. But when he began to lecture on
Ezekiel, instantly making us laugh, the lilt
and knife edge of Brittany in his Latin made it
too bright to see. I thought Master Peter spoke

only to me. A lightning wedding of eros and logos.
I was seventeen. In Paris. Dressed in blood velvet.
I had no felth that in our lives' weft and weaving
Medea's *naptha* was already threaded to poison us.

## Prime

I stood at girlhood's tent flap
in my shift, my sandals dangling
from one hand, and faced a phalanx
of Goliaths by the age of twenty,

armed with catapults a brute
necessity supplied. My pebbles felled
bombastic abbots, cardinals and kings.
Intelligence, my master archer,

fixed my aim, Defiance steadying my arm,
Contempt, a red-haired first lieutenant,
stocked my pouch with quartz. But
always at the front, an honor guard

who held the oriflamme, Desire leapt
to hurl the battle cry. *Submit, submit,*
the curlews called, unheard.
I strode ahead to meet the enemy,

forgetting how the aspen at the Rood
declined to bend her head on Calvary.
Children learn the aspen shakes
because she did not weep when

all Creation wept, and so her leaves
tremble always as punishment. Some
said it was pride that dunted me.
I was misunderstood as was the tree

that stood on Golgotha. The aspen saw
His Shadow cross the shadow of her arms,
according to His Wish, and she carried it.
She hardly heard the Sovereign's call to kneel,

thinking it was thunder. Wind and tumbling rain
eclipsed her sense. Paralyzed, earthfast,
she was condemned because her love refused
to look away. She only watched forsaken Jesus die,

his human voice more eloquent than God's.

## The Consolation of Boethius

I dreamt my love was lost, uncomforted.
He lay alone in Pavia, eclipsed
by fortune, by the catastrophic tides
of men, by Caesar's imminent collapse,

so long forgotten, left so long to grieve,
his body was its own sarcophagus,
the deep, impenetrable cell his grave.
Nothing moved but wind in starlit grass.

Insensibly, as mist across a marsh,
I came to weep with him and called his name,
my fingers swimming through a dreamer's mesh
too weak to drum his deafened tympanum.

Between the bars of summer moonlight, domed
like Saul on the Damascus Road, sheared
of custom, shorn of sense, my love lay damned,
despair his brutal, bloodless vanquisher.

His shadow seemed a white-haired Senator
who calmly bends above the bath he's drawn,
his last campaign a test of temperature
where courage and the taste of salt will drown,

who drops his tunic from his sword-scarred
flanks, the royal purple marbling with rose.
A cockroach jousting with a blot of ink
defiles his final parchment as it dries.

I saw his face search out the Pleiades,
his sockets guttering a prayer, for hope,
for consolation. When the spirit dies
before the flesh, it sheds a haunted shape.

His voice, beginning as a murdered oath,
refused to void the carnage he surveyed,
and suddenly it swelled to challenge death,
a trumpet on the pass at Roncevaux.

I hear him rail, "Give over, heart, and howl!
She will not come again. I site the shell
of Heaven's ear, in every shaft I hurl
Sophia—thousands do not dent the shield.

I wept in fever once until she came.
Her kisses quenched my burning heart,
she prayed, and with her tender lips' viaticum,
I lived, and wrote, the ghost of her reply.

But now indenture's thumbscrew, loved of saints,
a host of fiends and frenzies, undisguised,
collude and so beguile me from my sense,
the great circumference of the world is squeezed

into the skull I hold in both my hands.
My first and last companions, grief and rage,
defeated, dwindle down to candle ends
in hammered sconces Faith, the kitchen drudge,

forgot to douse. They blink contentedly
beside the crawling tankard and the crumbs.
Such little lamps to stay a constant law.
Too small to light the hardwood of my crimes.

Such tiny stars, extinguishing like snow
that flecks a dead love's hair. Twin sparks I place
midship. Two lanthorns that can't guide me now.
White noons that trespass on my darker peace.

Desire sighs upon the wicks, it fans
exhaustion, feathers up in hope, ascends
in fervent wing beats toward the rafters,
finds the scaffolded cathedral of my hands—

Sophia, Virgin, Sister, intercede!
You said ill fortune draws a man to God
with grappling hooks, but God has turned aside
and left me barbed and dangling at the gate.

I've wished for everything on earth and failed.
All writing burns. My words won't come again.
But I would give all language up to feel
some comfort from the shushing of your gown.

This fractured rooftree frets, the brightness stirs,
not with the suspiration of my prayer
but my breathless unbelief—those stars
are paper fixed in vaults of priories

that sparkle in the zodiac by day
but die by night, a mockery of stars.
Oh, God, I haven't got the heart to die,
or travel Heavenward on golden stairs.

I've lifted up my eyes and cannot see—
Sophia, where's salvation? What's my crown?"
He read the silence of the earth and sky,
and died, because he did not know I'd come.

from
*Magpiety*

*(2011)*

## Maudlin Speaks of Trees

When I was mad in Albion    the trees bent soft to care for me
I heard their singing boughs    wrapped as I was in dusk

and the hazel and the beech stood guard    their holy branches
hiding    holding me    as I stormed and thrashed    When I woke

I found I wore a dress    of hawthorn leaves    sewn with tiny thorns
The fairies' ashen combs    had teased the burdock from my hair

I lived to drink from a Druid's withy hands      In the *Life of St. Dunstan*
so they say    a harp sounded a song of joy    of its own accord

The oaks' feet reach deep into this England    this Albion    but it
was not my time to go down to that place    where no light ever comes

## Maud as a Maid

I once ran with milk-white legs    through brambled greenwood
dancing stone by stone    across the ache of a summer stream

clouds lowering darkly overhead    my body stitched together
with flying past hedges   witchery    and rain which crumpled my hair

I stopped with terror at the forest's edge    while the men took down
and dressed a doe   immense wet eyes delving me    the dark trees

leaned over their cutting    and the blood darkened    and I heard breathing
behind me under the oak    a boar    a wolf    and I was caught    between

blood and blood      and Heaven pressed its deepest Hell on me
a great sinner for a girl    and I fell out of the world without a sound

## Mad Maud's Complaint

The peregrines of winter rise    to clutch and shred the clouds
A plaguey poxy sun sinks    further into its sickbed ere it dies

Mortar in Bedlam's bricks    I've picked to powder with my nails
blows across the bridges in a squall    I cannot find my Tom

my merry Tom    whose madness fetters me here to grief
He's fled across the moors    a larrikin    to beg fleet-footed

from his manacles    gladly freed from his dishonest Maud
Did I dream his love astonished me    like pentecostal fire or

sibilants shook from trees    as he rhymed his melancholy airs or
I saw all at once    buds blush    flourish    fall from rose hips' flames

The Thames trembled with his voice    silvery it seemed to sing
my chilblained hands to silk again    my blackest feet clean and shod

I dreamt we'd married be    my Tom    sad Tom    merry Tom and me
He ran    wrenching with him    this world's motley in his wroth

His curses pierced my broken mind    I knew my roaring boy
no more    there's mist between us now    or murk    or vanishing

## Mad Maud and the Swans

The Keeper of the Queen's Royal Birds    in black and silver boots
his pikestaff like a pendulum    slicing through reeds    at the shore's edge

where we hide    barks good morrow to the mob-capped wives
twisting wet linens    and stretching them out flat to bleach on the bank

A pageant of swans    the breadth of the river    rides with the current
towards Gravesend like feathered schooners    as far as any eye can see

I lie back    my shift    petticoats    unbound hair    on the wet silk
light of the wavering tide    and the brightness holds me    rocking

until I know not sun    nor the day's breath    nor my arms' sprinkled skin
from the waves' cradle    When strands of lily pads twine my curls and try

to pull me under    my Tom wades in to carry me up    freeing a leech
from my throat    and we lie beside the other    on yellow stars of hawkweed

and white violets    which we crush with our flesh    We sleep or only dream
we sleep    What wakes us is a great swan parting the current like a prow

and suddenly long-necked Aphrodite    half-rises    lifts    opens immense
white wings over us    and all at once    the whole river is flying

not with the Queen's Royal Birds    but a shimmering eyrar of swans
I know are angels    soaring toward the day moon from the radiant Thames

from
# *Fifty-Two*

*(2007)*

## *Pictures*

Paul César Helleu used to borrow pen nibs from his friend Singer Sargent and do dry point portraits of society women in the *belle époque*. One inexplicably turned up in our cellar.

I live in a big black house. Whoever heard of a black house? I ought to laugh—and sometimes do. But I think a lot about the high windows in a gable under the slates.

## Routine

Tundra of the white paper. Steppes of emptiness and ice. Equipped
with crampons and picks, I notch out a poem on gneiss, frostbitten,
winded, afraid to die.
                              Between the typescript's withes and raddles,
soft-nostrilled animals of meaning poke inquisitive noses through caesuras,
enjambments, metaphor, to me. I lift a serif, duck under and enter the world.

## Imitation

Ravaged Magdalen, forgiven, long fingered by God to wander raggedly, discalced
and sun-stunned in the desert, weighed down by her hot, khamsin-sculpted hair—
what hubris to think Donatello knew me.

                            I'm housebound. Heavier than I've ever been.
Wholly immoblized. Shorn. Sealed in a seaside town deluged with storms since spring.
But the spirit, ah, of ironwood—rain-carved, starved into a tense, attenuated beauty.

## Changeling

Under the Muse's mothering marble arm and a boa of roses,
the lunette in shadow nearly as high as Olympus,
a sculpted maiden dreams—

                    but her toes are pink, wriggling,
impatient with thoughts of flight! The earth so beautiful—
and beckoning—and far—how can she help but jump?

## A Museum Piece

Flayed as Marsyas, my head throbs with waiting,
distracting me from the flensed tissue that bloodies
the virgin linen's underside—

I want flamenco,

two beaded McEwan's Ales, a friendly fuck,
not this painted canvas I've tried too hard to inhabit.

## A Saltbox in Vermont

Wood stove. Two desks kissing. Books. The latest in a series of sunset-colored dogs,
our tall sons, their stair-step children stamping off snow, the holiday table groaning
with our work: vegetables, poetry, merriment.

It never happened, the house, the oeuvre,
the husband holding me, older. Illness married me, first and forever, put me to bed
like a bad child. Daily, through rain's quicksilver, I count on an abacus of crows.

## At the Steps of the Widener Library

A girl my age laughs nearby, fresh from skiing in Zermatt, casual in her beauty, orthodontia, years of good breeding. Harvard Yard is milling with history, ideas, students garbed in confidence and cashmere.

                                     I stand unenrolled, smarts not trumping class.
I type at Toyota of Boston to keep my bed in a halfway house for the mentally ill.
In my one good dress I cross this compass rose for the bus, lacerated with light.

## Invitation

Yesterday I saw Caravaggio's *Bacchus*, his torso of ivory blushing with Eros,
offering me wine, fruit about to bruise, a wreath of grapes and maybe laurel.
I slapped the book shut, trembling.

                                       I feel a trace of fingerprints on me still, softer
than a brush of wet summer ferns, or mist coming in the window from the sea's
rough consecration. My loved ones will leave me. Nothing will go right again.

## A Story

Pre-Raphaelite hair, a little black dress and fuck-me pumps, my poems drawing
actors, dancers, painters to my Village digs; books, opera tickets, the Met.
Someone else is living the life I thought I'd get.

When I whistle, a white horse in Central Park
lifts his head, wickering. I lie down like Nebuchadnezzar to graze. My lips kissing
a subway grate two hundred miles away, years too late, his forelock whisks my cheek.

## The First Balmy Day

Winter undid me. I practiced in my dress of lime and ash being lost in the ossuary
of the cosmos, anonymous as mica, left for dead. Suddenly, a sprightly nurse,
some insistent Deirdre, bustles the windows up—

                                      the foam's aroma blowing in,
surf-roiled rocks like skulls in a tidal catacomb tumble at dawn and wake me.
I long to wade once in the sea with numinous Thalassa, washing morning clean.

## Enchantments

The Duc de Berry's Book of Hours took me years to read.
History brambled itself in my Celtic hair. So much myth
turned me caryatid—
                              who'll tear down this page, papyrus
like a scrim between us? I held myself away from earth too long.
Transfixed, I forgot to eat. To sleep. I forgot to let myself be loved.

## Glimpse

Isaiah's coal, ingested. Fear's voltage, enveined. Fingered, my past's
fractured tesserae. The future's encrypted thicket scryed—
my morning checklist stops the day.
                                        A colloquy of ducks in catkins,
the curriculum of clouds and estuary cormorants and gulls will easily follow—
if only I could learn to be at home in the world and with my kind.

## Ephemera

Dolphins fan the selkie's hair, a nightingale's tremolo
turns to amber in which a dragonfly wipes her eye, in which
Primavera's maidens gambol—
       here's how I walk with my cane:
on broken concrete, with carious teeth and barking with laughter.
Scarified. Shrunken. Childless. Shaking. Cruel.

## The Eater of Paper, the Drinker of Ink

With my pen point, I dig up the watermark, a white peony soft on my tongue.
In that sweet wafer I taste a cluster of birches, cherry, oak. I swallow acres
of forest, seed pods like limpets at my heart.

                                              The nib plunges into a black current.
Its unguent on my lips, I suck down the streets of Evangeline, the drowned parishes
of Katrina, these lines an alphabet drawn from a corpse's single alchemized hair.

## Library

Ballast, all my books, making me earthfast, each a clearing, a glade, a birch grove
where goddesses, governesses, girls like me frolic forever. Somewhere between
Graves and Hardy I'd hide, breathless to be read.

Pages, only panes of glass on loved worlds
denied me. Touching serifs' suffering as my own. Fingers on lips, a kiss' underside.
On each fly leaf an Em, my mark—a minim, a half-note, a half-life, the fiction of me.

## Farmers' Market

Summer's rainy gold splashes on pomegranates, pears,
pregnant women whose arms are abundant with bundles and babies,
tables in pyramids spilling with ripeness—

                                       the sunlight hurts my eyes,
the chirr of children piercing me. I sit. Fan myself. What do I have?
My mother dead. My heart unseeded. My bag of bitter oranges.

## In Florida

Did I tell you I sat out on my sister's porch in a hammock swing, watching
the evening cardinals weave her cherry laurel into a net of ribboned carmine silk,
convinced I'd live my life alone?
                              I saw Eros rise over the osiers, fletching an arrow
filched from Artemis' quiver and half-lifted up, only to meet his barb
of laughter. I sit back. First dusk comes on, then darkness, then the underworld.

## Fog

My self begins to vanish, cell by cell dissolving me until I disappear,
the pillow where I drowse unfeathering, the articulate world—whiter, whitest—
uncarving itself before my eyes.
                                   Pivot your heart to me, the stenciled firmament's
psalter says. Elongate the ley lines of your own white hand until you can, scrimshander,
etch back the shape of your being in air, poised between nothingness and the moon.

## Green Willow, Green Willow

Afloat on the current of petalled hair, her silk brocade is sinking,
her lips still madder-rhymed. Paisley silts her skin. I scold her
in Anglo-Saxon: it's hard and it hurts to die!
                                My body bucks. My mind in a scald of blood
skirts its riverbanks and cataracts, cramped. The plummeting heart
anchors, choked by the reeds of your artful, pretty death, Ophelia.

## Garden at Dusk

I dig them free, entombed in rye grass as they've been, my maiden roses,
and make a true bed for them, secateurs trimming their hair, shortening their skirts,
helping them enter this new century.

                                     Part of me too crosses the thorny turnstile
into summer where no summer has been. I only wish it was a boy actor stepping
from the night sky's wings, behind the mask of Agamemnon accusing me.

## Love in an Irish Family

Orphaned. Unmarried. Childless. No term for the worst of it—to be blackened by them,
losing so the young ones I cuddled and read to, the beaten flesh I kissed, blood's deep music.
I am unsistered now. Unbrothered.

                      I'll live. (*You've taken the East and the West from me.*)
In the beat between dusk and dawn. (*The sun and moon you've also taken.*)
In the breath between dusk and dark. (*You've taken God from me, if I'm not mistaken.*)

## Madrigal

Cocooned, my cabin, of wattle made. A pallet, a kettle, two feral cats. Afraid
of the whippoorwill. Even more of *elsewhere*. When you live solely on ink,
you begin to think you'll live on paper forever.

                        I heard a madrigal today and felt the universe split.
The sky shook out its silks and linens to dance! Oh, I want to fall in love with the earth.
I need your hands—open this massive mortal door so I can come out to you.

## How Much the World Weighs

Mahogany, majolica, silver, gold leaf, porcelain, bisque, brass, clawfoot everything, wrapped in newsprint, sheeting, steamer trunks and soot—all of it suffocatingly meant for me so she need never die.

What I want is two white rooms. Detachment. Light. To give her house away and go. To lift into, say, music. A single eighth note in an oboe solo. To leave nothing but bird bones and hair in the hairbrush behind.

## Beyond the Gifts of Aphrodite

Green as Chloe lying in the corn, I dreamt the fields opened and dark blue horses climbed for me. I did not know then I had a body, or could be loved, or would one day welcome the ancient parchment cheek of Hecate.

                         I will always lose months, estranged to myself, engaged to death. This is the year my throat's begun to sag, the chin to loosen, the mouth to curve down. Strange—I've never been able to sing more beautifully.

from

## *The Marsh Poems*

*(2011)*

## Casualty

for David Ferry

They carried him from the sea on his shield,
His greaves gushing what he thought were golden fish.

He did not know the ones who bore him
Nor which of Poseidon's horses frothed at their bits.

Asclepius rolled back his white sleeves.
There was incarnadine clotting the water,

Gouts of blood on the sandals of the stretcher-bearers.
There was nothing to be done.

They carried him across the moors, the mossy stones
    *Actium, Ardennes, Bannockburn, Borodino*

Along the marshy bank, the footpath rising up
    *Bosworth Field, Bull Run, Crécy*

Over the star-like daisies in the field grass of the vineyard
    *Constantinople, Corregidor, East Timor*

Beside the ivied trees under the theatre of the moon.
    *Damascus, Da Nang, Dresden, Dunkirk*

They carried him through the shady groves of the Great Plains,
    *Gallipoli, Hiroshima, Jerusalem, Kabul*

The murmuring of cypresses urging them on,
    *Kandahar, Khe Sanh, Leipzig, My Lai*

The stretcher-bearers printing the clay of Asia Minor
　*Nanking, Persepolis, Phnom Penh, Poitiers*

Through the tree trunks where the trail dissolved,
　*The Siege of Acre, the Siege of Austerlitz*

The mud now frozen ruts on mountainsides.
　*The Siege of Leningrad, Sarajevo, Solferino*

They followed the snowy lanes through sleepy villages,
　*Verdun, Vukovar, Wounded Knee*

They carried him under the rustling live oaks
(Cross over the river and rest in the shade)

Of elm and yews, the blue-gray mists of Shiloh
Drenching every decomposing grave.

## Phi

I could not find the Golden Bowl,
the Golden Bough, a golden wedding band;

I never saw the golden lights corona'd in
my children's hair, for they were not.

I longed to love and wept an ocean's worth
as decades ticked by, ticked by, and I

began to slice my heart and feed upon it
and turn away from every human face.

It happened then so fast, so bitterly:
golden molars in my mouth, a golden-headed cane,

and the tinkling brass that passes for gold
on the handles of the cheapest casket I could choose.

I wish I'd known before about the Golden Mean,
that my overbrimming heart was a nautilus,

and not alone, and had poured love out everywhere,
for Fibonacci so long ago had made me his,

and I was part of the world, and known, and loved
to the smallest coral moon on my smallest fingernail.

## Advent

Sparrows huddle in the hedges and the catherine wheel—
sinking in the December sky—darkness has yet to shatter.

So many stones in my mouth make me mute, prophecies
I try to utter won't be heard or believed, all for wanting to turn

away from the light of day. The gods are cruel in their rebukes.
Glyphs on my parchment skin read, *My heart will split before long.*

Look up at my window—my face in fever the same rose gold
as Trojan Cassandra's half-open lips, she who is so soon to die.

# Prophecy

*Virginia Woolf believed she was going mad*
*when she heard the birds speaking in ancient Greek.*

In leafy Bloomsbury, the pigeons are straining their collars.
They are printing out the rain's alphabet on the cobbles,

the muttering in their throats is the sound of water in gutters,
their utterance the consonants of Aeschylus. O Virginia, the birds!

As children, Cassandra and her brother slept the night in Apollo's
sanctuary and at dawn were found entwined by sacred snakes,

their tongues flicking the children's ears to clean them
so they could hear especially the voices of animals and birds,

and understand the divine language of nature. Listen!
The pigeons are describing you, and predicting your future.

## At the Marsh

Late June steams up from the estuary. A cormorant
bathes its wings in the blinding blue air. Heat, inaugurating

summer after so much rain, keeps touching my forehead,
a radiant benediction, an initiate's sweat pouring

from my devotions here. My hair is singed with light.
Salt hay scorches my feet. Mist lies down under the sun

to be consumed. Phragmites ignite. The beach roses blaze.
I'm sick and can't live long. I want to soak my marrow

in this cauldron, kindle each incandescent bone in earth's
hellfire banked with coals, and in this day's false cremation,

feel for an instant my final burning: the skin's sizzle,
crackling fat, my hair—a saint's burnished corona of flame.

## The First of July

West to east, bruise-colored clouds scud over the marsh.
I watch tidal pools darken to reveal emerging silver light.

All the gold has gone from the day. The hummock's salt hair
has turned gray overnight. When I hear bass notes of thunder

my legs curl under me. I become a treble clef drawn on
a white rock, transcribing the pitch of the sea as the line

of running swells west to east describes a musical stave.
I trace a ligature from cheek to clouds to summer's end.

In the iron-tasting, ionized air, a grace note of rain falls on
my wrist, the ripples' *glissando* repeating itself without rest.

# Gambits

for Ann Katz

I close my eyes and breathe. Words enter my body, gold chessmen
carved of flame that take their places on my black-and-white board.

I play against myself, but the contest declares itself older by far
than the Game of Kings. The pieces obey their own arcane rules:

shape-shifting bishops, rooks, knights promptly abandon the Court
for the wild—a burst of wings, fins, talons, tusks, eyeteeth, beaks.

It's a struggle to tame them. I can't out-think their tactics, tricks
or strategies. The game is over when pieces simply return to form:

figures of speech cover the page, lay claim to their spaces. When
no moves are left, I lay down my pen. That's how the Queen wins.

## Belle Isle

The air hangs heavy as wet sheets thrown over the line
of houses I can see if I squint at the marsh's farthest edge.

Saturated trees waver with heat, and red brick and tile roofs
shimmering in this sweltering day might be mistaken for a view

of Florence or Rome, minus the Duomo, the Baptistry, St. Peter's.
The murmuring, hallucinatory *trompe l'oeil* of this noon stuns me.

I could easily float away from my body. Closer, clearer is the back
of Belle Isle Cemetery where my friend Evy lies, her summer wings

dissolved like a dragonfly's under its burden of earth. We should still
be two school girls in that perpetual mosaic: heads close, her hand

cupped at my ear, whispering—through hair—the oldest secret.
The sun's brazier pours out greasy black smoke across the water

to signal *no election*. I could wait here forever on this red-tiled wall
for a white plume to appear and ascend, announcing the new pope.

# Widdershins

It's raining on the marsh but not on me. A midsummer sunshower
pocks the far-off brine at low tide. Beads of water

are strung in the air as though on harp strings from the fens
up to a bright break in the clouds. The shoals are empty of birds.

It's quiet, except for the crackling marram grass as the rain
turns windward, the mist blowing straight at me. The word

*trespass* come to mind—why now? The phragmites can't tell me,
nor the furrowed hummocks, exposed. You could drown here

if you walked out far enough. Nothing has turned out
as I thought it would. The harp has disappeared. A cowl of fog,

autumnal, covers my shoulders, blurs the marsh's edge.
Poor Ireland's dying, soon to be like Atlantis—a mythical place.

## Dog Days

Verdigris, rust, rot—even the sun is cirrhotic, phosphorescence
riding in uneasily on the agitated, late-summer tide. Skittering

egrets and sanderlings at the shoreline unthread the fraying hem
of the surf, their yellow beaks plucking at festering seaweed,

the bleached fists of starfish. The reeds are writing their wills.
Wind has given up braiding the white wisps of the salt hay's hair.

There's no telling when the weather will turn. There's isn't a place
in the world where I'm allowed to say—*I'm tired to death of life.* Gulls

circling overhead chastise me, the combers rise up, manes fuming.
Only sparrows in *rosa rugosa* are imploring, *Pity, have pity, let her go.*

## Madonna Hill

To the east, the ocean bellowing, silent container ships slice
the sky apart from the horizon, passing Graves' Light toward

the knot of islands in Boston Harbor. The marsh is waiting:
rock pools full of mercury and zinc, and the salt-fed sea grass,

exposed, a violent green. To the west at some distance and above
Orient Heights, a shrine to the Virgin is carved out of clouds.

Its crenellations of gold torn from the hillside mimic her crown.
Inside a six-ton copper and bronze statue rises over the pilgrims'

chapel underground. The Madonna stands barefoot on the globe
in all weathers, her veil and draperies in her embrace seem so light

as though all she carried might at any moment lift up in a sea breeze.
The sculptor, an Italian Jew saved by monks from the Nazis, modeled her

on the shroud of Turin, thinking a mother ought to bear a likeness
to her Son, but I've seen her, robust as any Tuscan peasant girl

trampling sun out of her father's grapes. From one side of the wide plaza
I study the cheek scarred by acid rain and find there marks of grief,

then, from the other side, she seems deeply suffused with love.
How strangely they've stationed her—not facing the city, the sea,

but, like a neighborhood saint accepting local gifts and supplications,
she shelters the brothers of Don Orione in their nursing home.

They call her *Madonna of the Universe*. Boston's crooked streets
are riddled with tobacco-colored rooms and tattered ochre shades.

Does her gaze ever find those shredded curtains like ghostly sails
luffing in the narcotic air of the crumbling Seaman's Mission?

## Chrismarium

Roses of Sharon, daubed with Impressionists' pink and mauve,
hug the last of the nineteenth century's porches, leaning out

over the little lanes that still remember the way to the sea:
*Neptune, Mermaid, Coral, Siren, Undine.* Over the sluggish town,

gray skies hang, a long-abandoned wedding tent.
*Who can light the windows of the dead?* Breakers keep trawling

rocks into troughs of rip tides, of undertow. I stand at the tip
of the island, salt's eternal burn anointing my forehead, lips.

I've forgotten all the prayers I ever knew. *Mea culpa.* I hear
as in a dream, *Rivers of grace, circle back to your fountainheads,*

*that each may run his course again.* And the surf's wheel
keeps churning the coastline's endless granite ossuary.

## Hurricane Season

The Queen Anne's lace is tatty, unmended. Pairs of paper whites
waltz by, settling in the silver-gray sea moss. It's dead low tide.

The breeze is stripped of its scents—not the stink of salt flats,
nor fish beached for miles at the shoreline, garotted in seaweed

and knots of raided mussel shells. This summer's defeat is total.
Over the marsh the air is charged, thunderheads already banked

above the causeway, battalions of indigo towers rolling in, blue
about to boil to black. Boat owners are pulling in their skiffs

and sailboats at little marinas the length of fractals on the coast.
In Winthrop, at the boulevard's crest, TV crews from Boston

are set to photo the furious Atlantic hurling itself at the seawall,
sending plumes sixty feet in the air, roaring in an arch the width

of the wide road, pounding cars and siding relentlessly in cataracts
of stones. By the time she hits full force, I'll be curled in bed inside

the howl—no longer counting heartbeats between booms of thunder
and the incandescence cracking the sky. Lightning's flashes of blue

powder will capture the marsh on nineteenth-century glass negatives.
A figure, wavering, surfaces in the transparency, wearing across

her shoulder like a quiver strap the mist of a colorless rainbow.
Wild sand runs from my hair, salt stings my lips. It is Irene—

both the hurricane and the goddess of peace in her chiton—
still as a caryatid awaiting the unappeasable storm's afterbirth.

## Foundering

My pencil leaves caterpillar scat on my lined page. Clouds
have tied the sun to the sky's rusted bed frame. The marsh

has withdrawn. No wind, no wading birds. A drowsy current
murmurs over hummocks of salt hay, in the dreams of sea grass.

Fat as a Buddha, I sit quietly and watch. First, the phragmites
bow like the newly confessed, the pallid salt moss picks its teeth,

young black-eyed Susans startle like school girls chastised
for whispering in class. This is all there is. All there ever is.

Me, trying to decline language onto canvas blank as tidal flats,
to open the estuary and fill the marsh's mouth with song.

## The First of January

The holidays done with, I can breathe again. Only this day
will be an endless rolling pasture of pristine snow, unmarked

but for a chickadee's delicate scrimshaw, a new field on which
I can hike into happiness and love without the torques my life

usually takes. This year will be different. Bright blue high tide
makes a little lake of the inlet. I sit on the bank above a clean page.

A laughing gull hovers high over the sea wall, a dripping clam tight
in his beak, letting fall the shell which breaks open on the salted rock.

He caws proudly, perhaps does chuckle as he picks at the belly.
A wheeling falcon waits in a thermal, eyes unerring and black. Then, fast

as a feathered shaft, he hits, gouges the gull's foolish white neck,
the hawk's jaw and talons killing the bird in one lethal shake.

Blood and flesh fly, flecks of it striping my hair and book. I shriek,
leaping up to slap off the gore, appalled—shocked to discover nature

could break in upon my reverie on nature. Suddenly, the afternoon's
turned dark, an auguring darkness I can't quite grasp, the phragmites

nodding by the dock as if to say, *What did you think?* Sharp pellets
of snow pierce my bare skin, and all at once, the marsh is unendurable.

Shivering, I duck into my collar and run for home, complicit,
the gull's carcass lying still and broken as the indigo dusk.

## Last Things

It passeth understanding, but the light *will* go out.
At the bedside, pure as an abbess, memory will rise

and escort her flesh and blood from your room.
No one will look back. They've already forgotten you.

The abyss like a nurse will press a gauze on your eyes
to quietly quench them, and they will be quenched.

The bones that loyally held you up will turn over
joint by joint, a marionette becoming its own kindling.

Skin so sweet in life to kiss will unwrap its parchment
cocoon, weightless as a spider's gossamer the slightest

puff of air will blow away. The ear's vibrating tympanum
by an angel's whisper will be sealed eternally in wax.

The mouth having lost all its words will gape open,
unsewn, your very name now a chimera. Somewhere

the earth is waiting, holding its breath. Will your beliefs
prove true? Rebirth? Reunion with the dead? Your essence,

incandescent in a galaxy of stars, merged with your dreams
of Heaven? What if the animal heart begs *for one more minute,*

fights for one more glimpse of day, and the self,
the final priceless spark, the mind's last ember,

which is laboring so hard not to be extinguished,
sees only nothingness, and is forever *put out, put out.*

## Forecast

*Raw, Dark, Dank, & Fog.* Surely, Dickensian lawyers
or the names of his invented Tyburn executioners.

*Whipstone Raw. Pinchbeck Dark. Frogspittle Dank. Cuffington Fog.*
This giddy fever makes me laugh out loud. Whoever they are,

they 're louring over my bedposts, one knotting rope for a noose,
one shaking open the hood, one hammering the scaffold,

the last assaulting the trapdoor with his worn-out boots.
In my dreamy state, I don't seem to mind. It's no more

than I deserve for all my transgressions. Toward daylight
they drag me out by my muddy shift. I blink in the sun.

But when I step barefoot onto the silvered splintery wood,
I suddenly pity my poor body which never instigated

any trouble in this world, my innocent foot walking
to its death at the hinge. Worse than dying is what will

surely follow, and here I sink to my knees: an autopsy—
carving and cracking open my ribs by technicians inured

to human fluids, organs, tendons, fat. I'll be lying cold
on their aluminum table. No beckoning celestial light,

only the swinging shade like a censer above their scalps,
the kind of lamp my father hung low like a tin tent

over a corrugated pen of baby chicks, once holding me up
under it to hear one feathery heart. I won't be warm again.

## Sojourn's End

I've been awhile away. They've mown the summer meadow.
Apple trees emerge beside the winter-tumbled granite wall

where morning glories run, as if in search of a shingled porch
and the trellis they once climbed. I've been awhile away.

I used to sit on the last of the narrow gauge's railroad ties
fallen from the roadside into the sand. It's streaked more

since the spring, now sepia and coppery-gold as it sinks
deeper into the sea grass. Near the tiny marina, the town

has placed a platform, bolting down a memorial bench
for the Tiernans, Arthur and Grace, whom I never knew.

A late sharp east wind herds the clouds like a collie,
their woolly shoulders colliding in confusion, turning

the current navy, then bright as they stumble and race
over hummocks and crab holes. I've seen a world here:

the widowed swan circling her dark reflection in a pool,
snowy egrets' yellow beaks nervously plucking the flats,

a great blue heron almost within reach, considering me
before lifting its wide Prussian blue- and slate-colored wings

and long stalk legs straight out behind it, the black toes
delicately pointed as the first ballet slippers of a child.

I've seen a hillside burning; *The Madonna of the Universe;*
heard the keen, elusive aria of the red-winged blackbird

as it suddenly flicked its way to where Evy lies. I've seen
gulls on patrol, salt hay gleaming in the sargassos of June,

lying down heat-struck in August, whispering with thirst.
I've eavesdropped on the gossip of phragmites and sumac.

I've watched winter rain rattling the waves out to sea, the tide
leaving its lace as an offering at my feet. I've been awhile away.

## Acknowledgements

*AGNI*: "A Story"; "Lauds"; "Leda Later"; an earlier version of *The Squanicook Eclogues*

*Best American Poetry* 1991, chosen by Mark Strand: "The Consolation of Boethius"

*Epiphany*: "Leda, Later"; "The Vigil"

*Fulcrum*: "Matins"

*Ibbetson Review*: "Hic Jacet"

*Jacket*: "A Salt Box in Vermont"; "Love in an Irish Family" appeared in an article written by Nora Delaney

*The Linen Way* (Rosa Mira Books, NZ, 2013): parts of "A January Poem"; "A Story"; "At the Steps of the Widener Library"; "Daphne in Mourning"; "Flight to Egypt"; "Green Willow, Green Willow"

*Little Star*: "Maudlin Speaks of Trees"; "Maud as a Maid"; "Mad Maud's Complaint"; "Mad Maud and the Swans"; "Phi"

*Nativity Poems* (FSG, 2001): "Flight to Egypt"

*New York Review of Books:* "Daphne in Mourning"; "Flight to Egypt"

*Paris Review*: "The Consolation of Boethius"

*Seven Poems from Daphne in Mourning, a Chapbook* (Pen & Anvil Press, 2010): "A Sparrow Fostered Elsewhere"; "Daphne in Mourning"

*Sewanee Review*: an earlier version of "Reply to Stryon"

*Sixty Years of American Poetry*: "The Consolation of Boethius"

*The Ottoman Estate*: "A Sea Change"; "Hic Jacet"; "In Florida"; "Invitation"; "Portrait of the Artist"

*Tuesday Poem*: "Leda, Later" in Tim Jones' "Books in the Trees" weblog; "Prophecy" in Janis Freegard's weblog

*Yale Review*: "Matryoshka"

Melissa Green is the author of several collections of poetry and two memoirs. She received the Norma Farber Award from the Poetry Society of America, and the Lavan Award from the Academy of American Poets. Her work has appeared in *AGNI*, *Little Star*, *Fulcrum*, and other journals.

ARROWSMITH is named after the late William Arrowsmith, a renowned classics scholar, literary and film critic. General editor of thirty-three volumes of *The Greek Tragedy in New Translations*, he was also a brilliant translator of Eugenio Montale, Cesare Pavese, and others. Arrowsmith, who taught for years in Boston University's University Professors Program, championed not only the classics and the finest in contemporary literature, he was also passionate about the importance of recognizing the translator's role in bringing the original work to life in a new language.

*Like the arrowsmith who turns his arrows straight and true,*
*a wise person makes his character straight and true.*

— Buddha

# Books by

# ARROWSMITH
PRESS